The Geologic Story of Mount Rainier

A look at the geologic past of one of America's most scenic volcanoes

Dwight R. Crandell

Alpha Editions

This edition published in 2021

ISBN : 9789355751485

Design and Setting By
Alpha Editions
www.alphaedis.com
Email - info@alphaedis.com

As per information held with us this book is in Public Domain.
This book is a reproduction of an important historical work. Alpha Editions uses the best technology to reproduce historical work in the same manner it was first published to preserve its original nature. Any marks or number seen are left intentionally to preserve its true form.

Contents

The Geologic Story of Mount Rainier — - 1 -

The Changing Landscape of 12-60 Million Years Ago — - 4 -

Thumbnail Biography of Mount Rainier — - 11 -

Results of Recent Eruptions — - 12 -

Why Glaciers? — - 23 -

Work Habits of Glaciers — - 26 -

Yesterday's Glaciers — - 30 -

Landslides and Mudflows— Past, Present, and Future — - 36 -

The Volcano's Future? — - 43 -

Further Reading in Geology — - 44 -

Footnotes — - 45 -

The Geologic Story of Mount Rainier

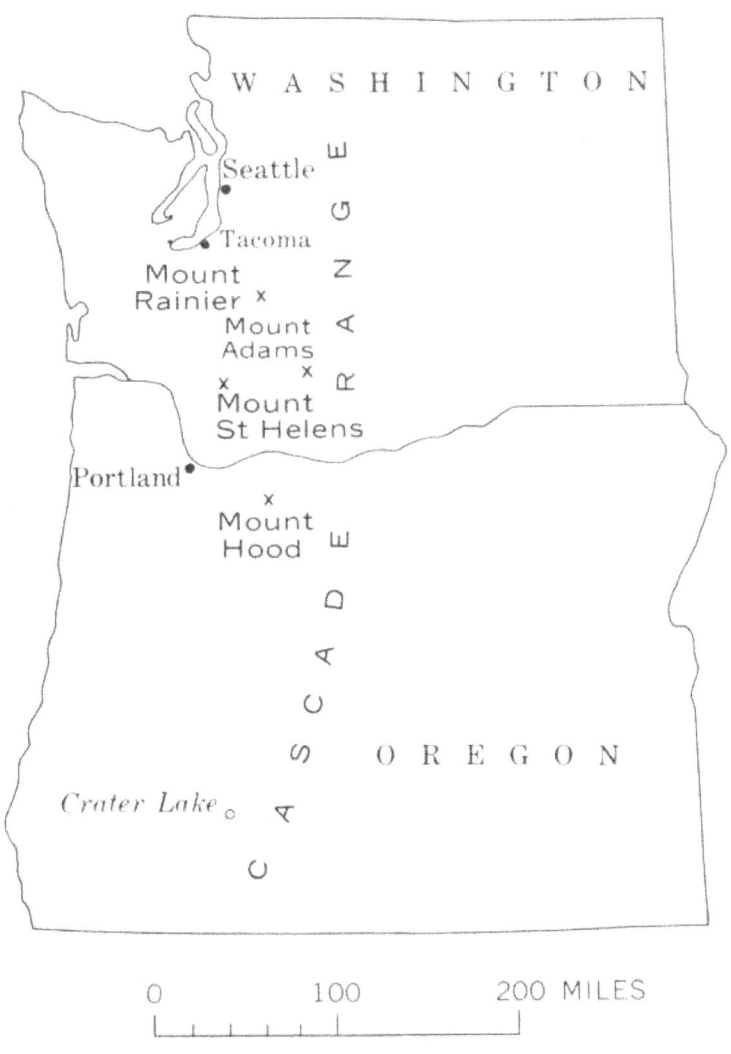

WASHINGTON

Seattle

Tacoma

CASCADE RANGE

Mount Rainier

Mount Adams

Mount St Helens

OREGON

Portland

Mount Hood

Crater Lake

Ice-clad Mount Rainier, towering over the landscape of western Washington, ranks with Fuji-yama in Japan, Popocatepetl in Mexico, and Vesuvius in Italy among the great volcanoes of the world. At Mount Rainier, as at other inactive volcanoes, the ever-present possibility of renewed eruptions gives viewers a sense of anticipation, excitement, and apprehension not equaled by most other mountains. Even so, many of us cannot imagine the cataclysmic scale of the eruptions that were responsible for building the giant 2 cone which now stands in silence. We accept the volcano as if it had always been there, and we appreciate only the beauty of its stark expanses of rock and ice, its flower-strewn alpine meadows, and its bordering evergreen forests.

Mount Rainier owes its scenic beauty to many features. The broad cone spreads out on top of a major mountain range—the Cascades. The volcano rises about 7,000 feet above its 7,000-foot foundation, and stands in solitary splendor—the highest peak in the entire Cascade Range. Its rocky ice-mantled slopes above timberline contrast with the dense green forests and give Mount Rainier the appearance of an arctic island in a temperate sea, an island so large that you can see its full size and shape only from the air. The mountain is highly photogenic because of the contrasts it offers among bare rock, snowfields, blue sky, and the incomparable flower fields that color its lower slopes. Shadows cast by the multitude of cliffs, ridges, canyons, and pinnacles change constantly from sunrise to sunset, endlessly varying the texture and mood of the mountain. The face of the mountain also varies from day to day as its broad snowfields melt during the summer. The melting of these frozen reservoirs makes Mount Rainier a natural resource in a practical as well as in an esthetic sense, for it ensures steady flows of water for hydroelectric power in the region, regardless of season.

Seen from the Puget Sound country to the west, Mount Rainier has an unreal quality—its white summit, nearly 3 miles high, seems to float among the clouds. We share with the populace of the entire lowland a thrill as we watch skyward the evening's setting sun redden the volcano's western snowfields.

When you approach the mountain in its lovely setting, you may find something that appeals especially to you—the scenery, the wildlife, the glaciers, or the wildflowers. Or you may feel challenged to climb to the summit. Mount Rainier and its neighboring mountains have a special allure for a geologist because he visualizes the events—some ordinary, some truly spectacular—that made the present landscape. Such is the fascination of geology. A geologist becomes trained to see "in his mind's eye" geologic events of thousands or even millions of years ago. And, most remarkable, he can "see" these events by studying rocks in a cliff or roadcut, or perhaps by examining earthy material that looks like common soil beneath pastureland many miles away from the volcano.

Our key to understanding the geology of Mount Rainier is that each geologic event can be reconstructed—or imagined—from the rocks formed at the time of the event. With this principle as our guide, we will review the geologic ancestry of this majestic volcano and learn what is behind its scenery.

The Changing Landscape of 12-60 Million Years Ago

The rocks of the Cascade Range provide a record of earth history that started nearly 60 million years ago. Even then, as today, waves pounded on beaches and rivers ran to the sea, molding and distributing material that formed some of the rocks we now see in the park.

You may find it difficult to imagine the different landscape of that far distant time. There was no Mount Rainier nor Cascade mountain range. In fact, there was very little dry land in the area we call western Washington. Instead, this was a broad lowland of swamps, deltas, and inlets that bordered the Pacific Ocean. Rivers draining into this lowland from the east spread sand and clay on the lush swamp growth. Other plants grew on the deposits, and they were covered, in turn, by more sand and clay. In this way, thousands of feet of sand and clay and peat accumulated and were compacted into sandstone, shale, and coal. We can see some of the rocks formed at that time in cuts along the Mowich Lake Road west of the park (fig. 1). Seams of coal were mined at Carbonado and Wilkeson, 10 miles northwest of the park, during the late 19th and the early 20th centuries.

These beds of sandstone, shale, and coal make up a sequence of rocks called the Puget Group, which is 10,000 feet thick. Wave-ripple marks and remains of plants show that the rocks were formed in shallow water fairly close to sea level. How could the rocks have piled up to this great thickness? The coastal plain and adjacent basin must have been slowly sinking, and the influx of sand and clay must have just barely kept pace with the downward movements.

Mount Rainier

[This map in a higher resolution]

A little less than 40 million years ago, the western Washington landscape changed dramatically. Geologists R. S. Fiske, C. A. Hopson, and A. C. Waters have discovered that volcanoes then rose on the former coastal plain at the site of Mount Rainier National Park and became islands as the area sank beneath the sea. When molten rock was erupted underwater from the submerged flanks of these volcanoes, steam explosions shattered the lava into countless fragments. The resulting debris, mixed with water, flowed as mud across great areas of the submerged basin floor.

Outcrop of gray to brown sandstone and dark-gray to black coaly shale in the Puget Group along the Mowich Lake Road. (Fig. 1)

You can see rocks formed from these layers of volcanic mud and sand in cuts along the highway on the east side of Backbone Ridge and between Cayuse Pass and Tipsoo Lake. Look there for alternating beds of grayish-green sandstone and breccia, a concretelike rock in which the pebbles have sharp corners. These rocks are known as the Ohanapecosh Formation. Like the Puget Group, the Ohanapecosh Formation is at least 10,000 feet thick. Yet, nearly all of it accumulated in shallow water as western Washington continued to sink slowly during the volcanic eruptions.

The long-continued sinking finally ended after the Ohanapecosh volcanic activity ceased. Western Washington was then lifted several thousand feet above sea level, and the Puget and Ohanapecosh rocks were slowly compressed into a series of broad shallow folds. Before eruptions began again, rivers cut valleys hundreds of feet deep, and weathering of the rocks produced thick red clayey soils similar to those that are forming in some areas of high rainfall and high temperature today. Look for the red rocks formed from these old soils in roadcuts as you drive along the Stevens Canyon road about 2 miles southeast of Box Canyon.

The next volcanic eruptions, which may have begun between 25 and 30 million years ago, differed from those of Ohanapecosh time. These volcanoes, somewhere beyond the boundaries of the park, erupted great flows of hot pumice that, being highly mobile, rushed down the flanks of the volcanoes and spread over many square miles of the adjacent regions. The pumice flows were "lubricated" by hot volcanic gas emitted from inside each pumice particle, which buffered it from other particles. Some hot pumice flows were 350 feet deep. The heat still remaining in the pumice after it stopped flowing partly melted the particles to form a hard rock known as **welded tuff**. Repeated pumice flows buried the hilly landscape and eventually formed a vast volcanic plain. The rocks, which are mostly welded tuffs, are now the Stevens Ridge Formation, which you can see along the highway in Stevens Canyon 1-2 miles west of Box Canyon. You can recognize the welded tuff by its light-gray to white color and its many flattened and sharp-edged inclusions of darker gray pumice (fig. 2).

Another period of volcanism followed, of still a different kind, when lava flowed outward from broad low volcanoes. The flows were of two kinds: basalt, the kind now erupted by Hawaiian volcanoes, and andesite, the type erupted by Mount Rainier. Individual flows 50-500 feet thick were stacked on top of one another to a total depth of fully 2,500 feet. We know these rocks as the Fifes Peak Formation. They form many of the cliffs and peaks in the northwestern part of the park. You can examine them in cuts along the Mowich Lake Road between Mountain Meadows and Mowich Lake. The time of the eruption of the Fifes Peak lavas may have been between 20 and 30 million years ago.

When the Fifes Peak volcanoes finally became extinct, this part of western Washington changed again. The rocks once more were uplifted and compressed into broad folds parallel to those formed at the end of Ohanapecosh time. The rocks buckled and, in places, broke and shifted thousands of feet along great fractures, or **faults**.

Outcrop of light-gray welded tuff in the Stevens Ridge Formation along the road in Stevens Canyon. The angular dark-gray fragments in the welded tuff are chunks of pumice. (Fig. 2)

About 12 million years ago one or more masses of molten rock, many miles across, pushed upward through the Puget Group and younger rocks. When this molten rock cooled and hardened, it formed granodiorite, a close relative of granite. Although most of the molten rock solidified underground, some of it reached the land surface and formed volcanoes at a few places within the area of Mount Rainier National Park.

Granodiorite looks like granite and has a light-gray speckled appearance. The knife is about 3 inches long. (Fig. 3)

Granodiorite is probably the most attractive rock in the park. It is mostly white, but it contains large dark mineral grains that give it a "salt-and-pepper" appearance (fig. 3). The large size of the grains is a result of the molten rock cooling slowly at a considerable depth below the land surface—the individual minerals had a long time to grow before the "melt" solidified into rock. In contrast, the rocks formed from lavas that flowed onto the ground surface are generally fine grained because the lavas cooled too quickly for the mineral grains to grow appreciably.

Granodiorite underlies the White River valley, the Carbon River valley, and parts of the upper Nisqually River valley and the Tatoosh Range. You can see it in roadcuts between Longmire and Christine Falls and at several places along the road between White River Ranger Station and White River campground.

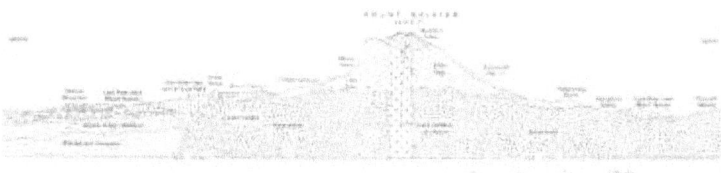

Geological cross section of Mount Rainier and its foundation rocks from Mother Mountain southward to Tatoosh Range. True-scale cross section is nearly 17 miles long. Slightly modified from U.S. Geological Survey Professional Paper 444, Plate 1. (Fig. 4)

(left) **High-resolution Diagram** *(right)*

After the granodiorite solidified, the foundation of Mount Rainier was complete except for one other landscape change that preceded the birth of the volcano. Not long after the granodiorite was formed, the Cascade mountain range began to rise—not rapidly, but little by little over many thousands of years. As the land rose, rivers cut valleys into the growing mountains so that by the time the new volcano began to erupt, the Cascades had already been carved into a rugged range of high ridges and peaks separated by deep valleys. Deep erosion thus laid bare the rock layers in which we today read the geologic history of the park (fig. 4).

Thumbnail Biography of Mount Rainier

The life span of a volcano can be compared to that of an individual—after his birth and a brief youth, he matures and grows old. The birth date of Mount Rainier is not known for sure, but it must have been at least several hundred thousand years ago. We cannot tell much about the volcano's complex youth because most of its earliest deposits are now buried under later ones. At an early age, well before the cone grew to its present size, thick lava, like hot tar, flowed repeatedly 5-15 miles down the deep canyons of the surrounding mountains. Because these lava flows resisted later erosion by rivers and glaciers, most of them now form ridgetops, as at Rampart Ridge, Burroughs Mountain, Grand Park, and Klapatche Ridge (figs. 5 and 6). Violent explosions occasionally threw pumice onto the slopes of the growing volcano and the surrounding mountains. As the volcano matured, the long thick flows were succeeded by thinner and shorter ones which, piled on top of one another, built the giant cone that now dominates the region. Even though Mount Rainier has grown old now, it has revived briefly at many times during the last 10,000 years or so and may erupt again in the future.

The events of the last 10,000 years, because they are so recent, in terms of geologic time, are better known than those of any earlier time, and we can examine this part of the volcano's history in some detail. We will study three principal subjects: eruptions—because they have had widespread effects; glaciers—because they are such conspicuous features on the mountain; and landslides—because they have drastically changed the volcano's shape.

Results of Recent Eruptions

While hiking, you soon become aware that there is a large amount of pumice along the trails in Mount Rainier National Park. Pumice is a lightweight volcanic rock so full of air spaces that it will float on water. The air spaces, or bubbles, originated when fragments of gas-rich lava were explosively thrown into the air above the volcano, and the molten rock hardened before the gas could escape. If you examine pumice deposits in a trail cut, in a streambank, or in the roots of blown-over trees, you may also note that there is more than one layer (fig. 7). If you circle the volcano on the Wonderland Trail, you may notice that the greatest number of pumice layers are on the east side of the park, but the thickest single layer is on the west side. The explanation lies partly in the source of the pumice deposits, because some pumice was erupted not by Mount Rainier but by other volcanoes in the Cascade Range of Washington and Oregon and brought to the park by strong southerly or southwesterly winds. The layers of pumice thrown out by Mount Rainier within the last 10,000 years lie mostly on the east side of the volcano. Strong winds evidently swept eruption clouds to the east during the outbursts and prevented the pumice from falling west of the volcano. This pattern of distribution, coupled with the coarsening and thickening of the pumice toward the volcano, reveals that the layers were erupted by Mount Rainier.

An old lava flow from Mount Rainier which forms Rampart Ridge west of the meadow at Longmire. The thick lava flowed down an old valley floor and cooled and solidified. Rivers then eroded new valleys along both sides of the flow. These new valleys, subsequently glaciated, are today followed by the Nisqually River and Kautz Creek. Thus, the area of a former valley floor is now a ridge. (Fig. 5)

Columns of dark-gray andesite at the east end of an old lava flow from Mount Rainier. This outcrop is near the point at which the highway to Yakima Park crosses Yakima Creek. (Fig. 6)

Layers of pumice on the floor of a cirque near Paradise Park. The yellow bed at the bottom is layer O, which was erupted by Mount Mazama volcano at the site of Crater Lake, Oregon, about 6,600 years ago. The yellowish-brown layer a few inches above layer O is layer D, a pumice that was erupted by Mount Rainier between 5,800 and 6,600 years ago. The light-yellowish-brown pumice bed at the top of the outcrop is layer Y, which originated at Mount St. Helens volcano between 3,250 and 4,000 years ago. Photograph by D. R. Mullineaux, U.S. Geological Survey. (Fig. 7)

D. R. Mullineaux of the U.S. Geological Survey has studied in detail the pumice deposits of Mount Rainier National Park. One of his first and most important discoveries was that even though some pumice layers are spread widely over the park, they were erupted from other volcanoes. Strangely enough, one layer is thicker and more widespread than any recent pumice erupted by Mount Rainier. We can clearly see that these foreign pumice layers did not come from Mount Rainier, for they thicken and coarsen southward, away from the park. The oldest was erupted by Mount Mazama volcano at the site of Crater Lake, Oregon, about 6,600 years ago; this pumice forms a yellowish-orange layer about 2 inches thick nearly everywhere in the park. The pumice has a texture like that of sandy flour, and it feels grainy when rubbed between the fingers. It is so fine grained because of the great distance to its source, 250 miles due south of Mount Rainier. Near Crater Lake this same pumice consists of large chunks and is many feet thick.

Two other foreign pumice deposits in the park were erupted by Mount St. Helens, a symmetrical young volcanic cone about 50 miles southwest of Mount Rainier. The older of the two is between 3,250 and 4,000 years old; it forms a blanket of yellow sand-sized pumice that is as much as 20 inches thick in the western part of the park. The younger pumice layer is most conspicuous at the ground surface in the eastern part of the park, where it is as much as 4 inches thick and resembles a fine white sand. It is about 450 years old.

Mount St. Helens as it appears from Mount Rainier.

An inconspicuous bed of pumice records the first eruption of Mount Rainier that occurred after Ice Age glaciers melted back to the slopes of the volcano. It can be found on the east side of the mountain from Grand Park south to Ohanapecosh campground (fig. 8). In roadcuts near the east end of Yakima Park (Sunrise) the pumice forms a rusty-brown bed about 4 inches thick which contains fragments as much as 2 inches across. Wood from a thin layer of peat just above the pumice was dated by its content of radioactive carbon as about 8,750 years old; thus, the pumice is even older. We call this pumice layer R for convenience; other letter symbols have been assigned to the younger layers (table 1).

Generalized distribution of some pumice layers within Mount Rainier National Park. The pumice of layers W and Y was erupted by Mount St. Helens; all the other pumice originated at Mount Rainier. Letters represent the following localities: C, Cougar Rock campground; I, Ipsut Creek campground; L, Longmire; M, Mowich Lake; O, Ohanapecosh campground; P, Paradise Park; S, summit crater; T, Tipsoo Lake; W, White River campground; and Y, Yakima Park. Based on studies by D. R. Mullineaux. (Fig. 8)

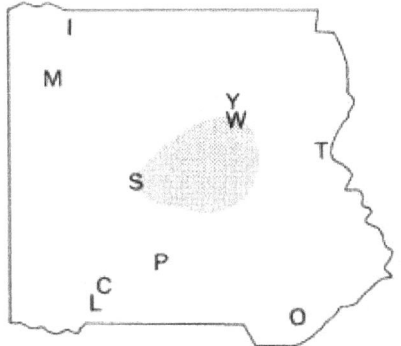

Layer X (Between 110 and 150 years old)

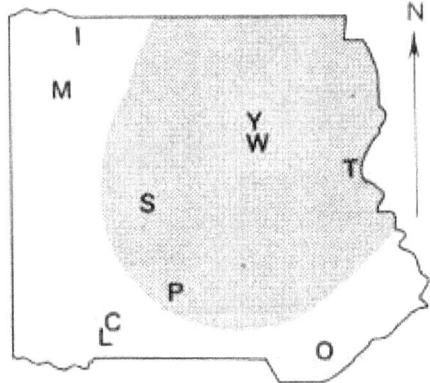

Layer C (Between 2,150 and 2,500 years old)

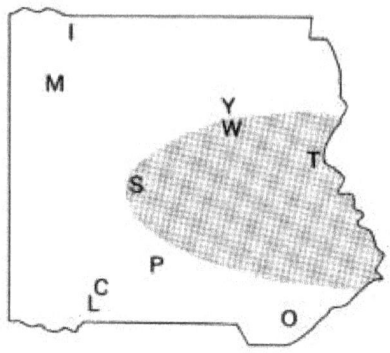

Layer D (Between 5,800 and 6,600 years old)

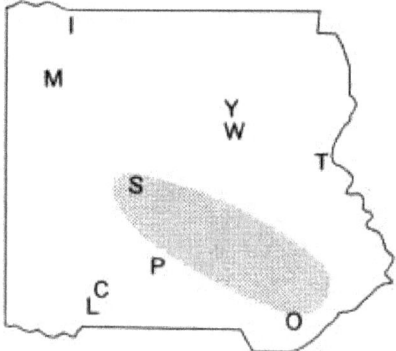

Layer L (Between 5,800 and 6,600 years old)

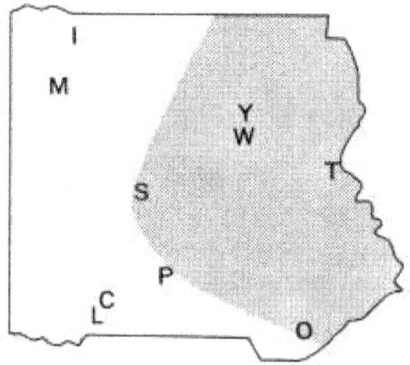

Layer R (More than 8,750 years old)

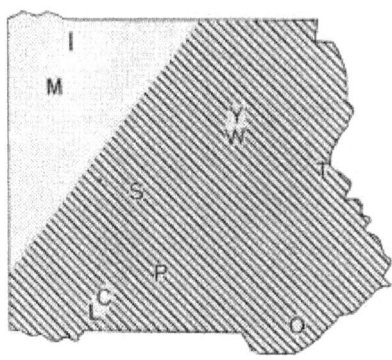

Layer W (line pattern), and Layer Y (stipple pattern) (About 450 years old and 3,250 to 4,000 years old, respectively)

TABLE 1.—*Characteristics, sources, and ages of pumice layers, Mount Rainier National Park*
[Based on studies by D. R. Mullineaux]

Pumice layer	Common range of thickness in park West side (inches)	East side (inches)	Common range in diameter of pumice fragments (inches)	Color	Source	Approximate age in 1968, or limiting dates (years ago)
X	Absent	[1]	¼-2	Light olive gray	Mount Rainier.	100-150
W	0-1	1-3	Medium sand	White	Mount St. Helens.	[2]450
C	Absent	1-8	¼-8	Brown	Mount Rainier.	2,150-2,500
Y	5-20	1-5	Coarse sand	Yellow	Mount St. Helens.	3,250-4,000

D	Absent	0-6	¼-6	Brown	Mount Rainier.	5,800-6,600	
L	Absent	0-8	¼-2	Brown	Mount Rainier.	5,800-6,600	
O	1-3	1-3	Flourlike to fine sand	Yellowish orange	Mount Mazama.	About 6,600	
R	Absent	0-5	⅛-1	Reddish brown	Mount Rainier.	8,750-11,000?	

The next two eruptions of Mount Rainier occurred between 5,800 and 6,600 years ago. Again, pumice spread over the area east of the volcano. The older pumice, which we call layer L, covers a band only a few miles wide that extends to the southeast from the volcano (fig. 8). The younger pumice, layer D, covers an area at least 10 miles wide directly east of the volcano. The distribution of both deposits shows that there were strong directional winds during the eruptions. The long, narrow pattern of layer L probably was caused by strong northwesterly winds during a short-lived eruption. The pattern of layer D was caused by winds from the west.

Some time during these eruptions, hot volcanic bombs and rock fragments were thrown out of Mount Rainier's crater and fell onto surrounding areas of snow and ice. Wholesale melting resulted, and floods descended the east flank of the volcano carrying millions of tons of ash, newly erupted rock debris, and breadcrust bombs. Breadcrust bombs seem to be solid rock, but if you would break one open, you would find that the inside is hollow or is filled with a spongy mass of black glass. Their outer surfaces are cracked like the crust of a loaf of hard-crusted bread (fig. 9), so we call them **breadcrust bombs**. They originated as blobs of soft, red-hot lava which were thrown out of the volcano's crater. As the masses arched through the air, they quickly chilled on the outside, and a hardened skin formed around the still hot and plastic core. As their outsides cooled, gas pressure in their hot interiors caused the bombs to expand slightly and their solidified outer skin to crack. When they struck the ground, many of the bombs became flattened on one side, but they were still plastic and sticky enough to remain whole.

Bombs can be found in two deposits that form the south bank of the White River about half a mile downstream from the White River campground. The deposits are **mudflows** caused by the mixing of hot rock debris with the water from melted snow and ice. As the mudflows moved down the valley floor they must have resembled flowing masses of wet concrete.

Mount Rainier erupted several times between about 2,500 and 2,000 years ago. During one of the first eruptions, a mass of hot ash, rock fragments, and breadcrust bombs avalanched down the side of the volcano and buried the floor of the South Puyallup River valley. Although this hot mass flowed like a wet mudflow, the temperature of the rock debris was above 600°F. Thus, if any water had been present, it would have been in the form of steam. You can see the resulting deposit in cuts along the West Side Road on both sides of the bridge across the South Puyallup River. Innumerable bombs have rolled from the cuts into the ditches beside the road. A charcoal log found in the deposit had a radiocarbon age of about 2,500 years.

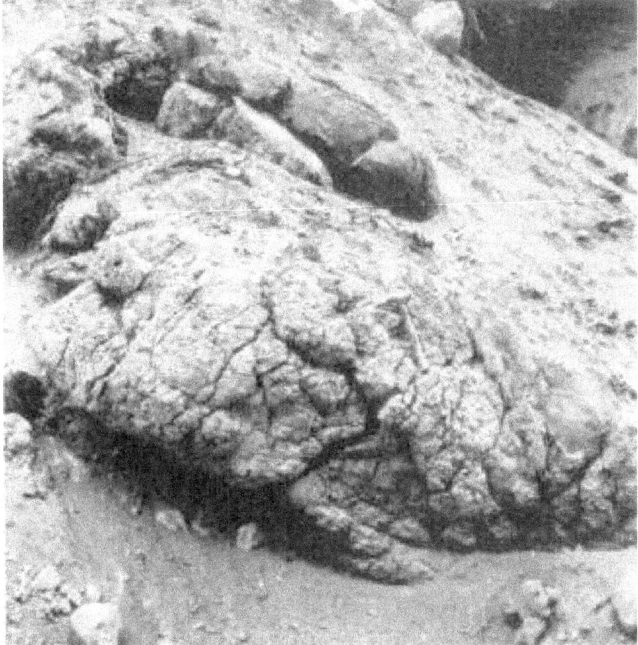

A large breadcrust bomb enclosed in a mudflow deposit that consists of a mixture of volcanic ash and rock fragments. The outcrop is on the south bank of the White River about half a mile downstream from the White River campground. (Fig. 9)

Large amounts of pumice were thrown out of the volcano at the same time as the bombs or soon after. The pumice covers most of the eastern half of the park, and fragments are scattered as far southwest as Pyramid Peak and as far northwest as Spray Park. This pumice, called layer C, is especially thick and coarse at Yakima Park and Burroughs Mountain, where it lies at the ground surface (fig. 10). Here the light-brown layer is 5-6 inches thick and consists of irregularly shaped pumice fragments as much as several inches across. Mingled with the pumice fragments are fist-sized chunks of light-gray rock that probably were simultaneously thrown out of the volcano by violent explosions. Some of these angular rocks were hurled as far as Shriner Peak, 11 miles east of Mount Rainier's summit.

Pumice layer C, which consists of light-brown fragments, lies at the ground surface over much of the eastern part of the park. (Fig. 10)

The eruptive period was climaxed by the building of the volcano's present summit cone, which is at least 1,000 feet high and 1 mile across at its base. Although dwarfed by the tremendous bulk of Mount Rainier, it is a little larger than the cone of the well-known Mexican volcano Parícutin that appeared in 1943 and erupted until 1952. Mount Rainier's present summit cone was built within a broad depression at the top of the main volcano that had been formed nearly 4,000 years earlier (fig. 11; see p. 40). The cone consists of a series of thin black lava flows, and its top is indented by two overlapping craters. Rocks around the craters are still warm in places, and steam vents melt caves in the summit icecap. The first climbers who reached the top of the mountain, in 1870, spent the night in one of these caves, as have many benighted climbers since.

The snow-covered lava cone lies in a depression 1¼ miles wide at the summit of the volcano. The cone was probably built about 2,000 years ago. Liberty Cap is to the left and Point Success is to the right. The cliffs below and to the right of Liberty Cap enclose Sunset Amphitheater. (Fig. 11)

Even though the lava flows that formed the summit cone were relatively short, their eruption greatly affected some valleys at the base of the volcano. The hot lava melted snow and ice at the volcano's summit, causing floods that rushed down the east and south sides. When the floods reached the valley floors, they picked up great quantities of loose rock debris and carried it downstream, sometimes forming mudflows. The resulting flood and mudflow deposits raised the floors of the White and Nisqually River valleys as much as 80 feet higher than they are today. These valley floors, as well as several others, then became broad wastes of bare sand and gravel that extended beyond the park boundaries. Later, the rivers cut down to their present levels, but they left remnants of the flood and mudflow deposits as terraces or benches along the sides of the valleys. You can camp on such a terrace in the Nisqually River valley at the Cougar Rock campground. The White River campground occupies a similar terrace in the White River valley.

When did Mount Rainier erupt last? The most recent pumice eruption was just a little over a century ago. However, between 1820 and 1894, observers reported at least 14 eruptions. Some of these may have been just large dust clouds, caused by rockfalls, that were mistaken for clouds of newly erupted ash. Other clouds may have been from genuine eruptions that left no recognizable deposits. D. R. Mullineaux has found that at least one eruption of that era did spread pumice over an area east of the volcano between Burroughs Mountain and Indian Bar to a distance of at least 6 miles from the crater. Pieces of the pumice, layer X, are light brownish gray and as large as 2 inches across. We find only scattered fragments of the pumice, and nowhere are they in a continuous layer. Where the X pumice is directly on top of layer C, we cannot tell them apart. The best areas for us to study the younger pumice, therefore, are glacial moraines formed within the last 150 years, because no pumice other than layer X is present on the moraines. Fortunately, R. S. Sigafoos and E. L. Hendricks of the U.S. Geological Survey have determined the ages of the moraines by counting the growth rings of trees on them. Their studies show that the pumice was erupted between about 1820 and 1854.

Captain John Frémont, an early explorer of the Oregon Territory, recorded that Mount Rainier was erupting in November 1843, but his journals give no details. Others have reported eruptions in 1820, 1846, 1854, and 1858. Pumice layer X probably was erupted during one or more of these times, but we do not know exactly when.

And will Mount Rainier erupt again? We think that it will, but we now have no sure way of predicting the time, the kind, or the scale of future eruptions.

Why Glaciers?

We frequently hear the question: "Why are there glaciers on Mount Rainier?" A glacier forms wherever snowfall repeatedly exceeds melting over a period of years. Above 6,500-7,000 feet on Mount Rainier, more than 50 feet of snow falls each winter, and not all of it melts before the next winter. The survival of this snow from one year to the next depends partly on the cooler temperatures at the higher altitudes, and perhaps also on the somewhat deeper snowfalls there.

Two ice streams meet to form the half-mile-wide Cowlitz Glacier. One heads on the flank of the volcano and the other (Ingraham Glacier) at the summit. The firnline is a short distance above the junction of the glaciers. The high bare embankment at the extreme right is a lateral moraine that was formed about 100 years ago when the glacier was thicker and about 1½ miles longer. (Fig. 12)

LITTLE TAHOMA PEAK

MOUNT RAINIER

INGRAHAM GLACIER

COWLITZ GLACIER

A line that marks the limit on a mountain above which snow persists from one winter to the next is called the **annual snowline**, and this line on a glacier is called the **firnline** (fig. 12). Above the firnline, snow that falls each year packs down and changes into glacier ice as air is slowly forced out of it. This part of the glacier is its accumulation area, where more snow falls each year than is lost by melting. Below the firnline is the ablation area, where melting predominates. The firnline on Mount Rainier's glaciers has been well above 6,500 feet in recent years. But some glaciers extend to altitudes below 5,000 feet—that is, far down into the ablation area. They do this by slowly flowing downhill. Solid ice flows by sliding on the hard bedrock under the glacier and by slipping along the innumerable surfaces within the ice crystals that make up the glacier.

The rate of flow and the rate of ablation govern the distance a glacier extends down into the ablation zone. If these rates remain fairly constant, the glacier will be in balance and its size will be about the same from year to year. But if changing weather patterns affect the rates of ablation or accumulation, or both, the glacier will either become smaller or grow larger. The change you are most likely to notice is in the position of the glacier's terminus, which may either recede or advance, but precise measurements of the upper reaches of a glacier also show volume changes there, some of which may not affect the glacier's terminus for many years, if ever.

Crevasses are a glacier's most awesome features and are a constant hazard for climbers. They form where adjacent parts of a glacier are moving at different speeds. Some of Mount Rainier's glaciers may be flowing at a speed of several thousand feet per year along their centers but at a much slower rate along their margins. This unequal rate of flow produces stresses in the ice that cause it to break. Groups of crevasses often form where the glacier flows over a steep place in its bed. The ice moves faster here, and pulls apart, and a crevasse is formed. Although a large crevasse may seem to be bottomless to the observer, most crevasses are less than 100 feet deep because ice pressure tends to close the open spaces in the ice below that depth.[3]

Ice covers 37 square miles of the park today. Individual glaciers that make up this ice blanket are placed into three groups, depending on their place of origin. Those of one group originate at the volcano's summit and flow far down the valleys that radiate from the cone. Most of the snow that nourishes these glaciers probably falls on them at altitudes well below the summit. The largest examples of the group are the Emmons, Nisqually, and Tahoma Glaciers.

Glaciers of the second group originate on the flanks of the volcano, mostly at altitudes between 7,000 and 10,000 feet. This group is represented by the South Tahoma, Carbon, and Inter Glaciers. Glaciers of the third group are on north facing slopes in the mountains around Mount Rainier. They are mostly at altitudes of about 6,000 feet, and they owe their existence to locations well protected from solar heat. Glaciers representing this group are the Unicorn and Pinnacle Glaciers in the Tatoosh Range, a small unnamed glacier near the west end of Burroughs Mountain, and the somewhat larger Sarvent Glaciers east of Mount Rainier.

Work Habits of Glaciers

Glaciers are extremely capable workers. Their work includes **erosion, transportation, and deposition**. The smoothed and grooved bedrock at Box Canyon and at many points along the trail to the ice caves near Paradise Park shows erosion of rock by glacier ice. Rock fragments carried by glaciers cut grooves in the hard bedrock and polish its surface (fig. 13). Although any one rock fragment might scrape away only 1 millimeter of rock along a single groove, the total effect is great when multiplied by countless thousands of similar fragments rasping a bedrock surface for hundreds or thousands of years. Glacier ice may also break chunks of rock loose as it overrides them and may even plow up sections of softer rocks.

Glaciers transport not only the rocks that they quarry and scrape from their beds but also, more conspicuously, those that fall onto their surfaces from nearby cliffs. These falling rocks range in size from tiny particles to individual masses that weigh tens of thousands of tons, like those that fell onto Emmons Glacier from Little Tahoma Peak in 1963. (See p. 35.)

A glacier deposits most rock debris at its terminus. The steep snout of any major glacier is a dangerous place to approach closely because rock debris almost constantly falls, rolls, and slides down the melting ice faces. Much of this debris collects at the ice margin, and if the margin stays in one place long enough a ridge-shaped **end moraine** of rock debris forms along the ice front (fig. 14). If such a moraine forms across the front of a glacier at its farthest advance it is called a **terminal moraine**. End moraines that form as the ice recedes are called **recessional moraines** (fig. 15). Ridges of rock debris that form along the sides of a glacier are called **lateral moraines** (fig. 12).

Some recent moraines of modern glaciers are only a few feet away from the present ice margin; others, formed thousands of years ago during the most recent major glaciation, are on ridgetops and valley sides or floors miles away from modern glaciers. By examining the shape and location of these moraines, we can reconstruct the size and character of past glaciers, as we will see in the next section.

Glacier-smoothed and grooved rock along the Wonderland Trail between Indian Bar and Panhandle Gap. (Fig. 13)

A muddy grayish-blue lake several hundred feet long lies behind a small horseshoe-shaped end moraine of Flett Glacier, on the northwest side of Mount Rainier. The glacier is mostly out of view to the left. (Fig. 14)

Glaciers erode, transport, and deposit huge quantities of rock debris. So do their coworkers, the melt-water streams. These turbulent streams flow from tunnels beneath every glacier, and their degree of muddiness roughly shows how active the glacier is. Glaciers that move very slowly, or that are stagnant, produce relatively clear melt water because they are not actively eroding bedrock. In contrast, streams of muddy water that look like chocolate milk often come from very active or "live" glaciers. These streams carry rock debris ranging from flour-size particles to large boulders. You can sense the carrying power of this swiftly moving water on warm summer days, when large cobbles and boulders are bumping along in a stream swollen by rapid glacier melting. Although you can rarely see these boulders, you can hear their constant low thunder. Their repeated impacts on other boulders in the streambed will vibrate the nearby streambanks beneath your feet. Hikers often find that a melt-water stream safe to cross in the early morning of a warm summer day is an impassable torrent at the same spot by early afternoon.

Four curved recessional moraines are spread over a distance of 2,000 feet on the valley floor of Fryingpan Creek. They were formed within the last few hundred years as Fryingpan Glacier lost volume and shrank back toward its present position above a line of cliffs. (Fig. 15)

A melt-water stream generally deposits coarse material wherever the slope of the valley floor decreases and the stream loses some of its velocity and carrying power. Only a flood may move the boulders farther downstream. However, the current carries fine material far downstream to deposit it in lakes, in Puget Sound, or in the Pacific Ocean. The Puyallup River, for example, is still very muddy where it enters Puget Sound at Tacoma, more than 40 miles from its source in the glaciers on Mount Rainier.

During the last glaciation, when glaciers were much larger than they are now, melt-water streams carrying great quantities of sand and gravel built valley floors up to levels tens of feet higher than they are today. Later, as the glaciers grew smaller, the rivers cut down into their valley floors and remnants of the sand and gravel deposits were left standing in benches or terraces along the sides of the valleys. You can see a good example of such a terrace in the Nisqually River valley beyond Ashford, which is 5 miles west of the park. You cross it on the highway that leads to the park. Cuts beneath the terrace reveal deposits of sand, cobbles, and boulders that look the same as those deposits being formed today by melt-water streams. The terrace west of Ashford was formed a little more than 15,000 years ago, when a glacier extended down the Nisqually River valley to the vicinity of Ashford.

Yesterday's Glaciers

Mount Rainier's great sprawling cone would seem incomplete without the glistening sheets of ice that descend its flanks. We have reason to believe that the volcano has borne glaciers ever since its origin—sometimes smaller than now, at other times vastly larger. Mount Rainier probably started to grow during the middle part of the Pleistocene Epoch, or Ice Age, which began more than 1 million years ago, but glaciers had covered this part of the mountains even before the volcano appeared. Masses of rock debris formed by ancient glaciers occur beneath lava flows from Mount Rainier on the west side of Mazama Ridge just upslope from Narada Falls, on the north side of Glacier Basin, and at a few other places in the park.

Mount Rainier may have reached its present size by about 75,000 years ago. Since that time great icefields and glaciers have formed at least three times on the slopes of the volcano and in the nearby mountains. During the first two glaciations, ice completely buried the flanks of the volcano and the surrounding mountains, except for the very highest ridges and peaks. These great ice masses slowly flowed down all the valleys that head at Mount Rainier. The glacier in the Cowlitz River valley, for example, extended 65 miles from the volcano and reached a point about 33 miles west of the community of Randle. Deposits of the younger of these two glacial episodes can be seen in cuts along the Mowich Lake Road for a distance of about 1½ miles inside the park boundary. The glacial deposits were originally more widespread, but in most of the park they have been removed by erosion or covered by the deposits of yet younger glaciers.

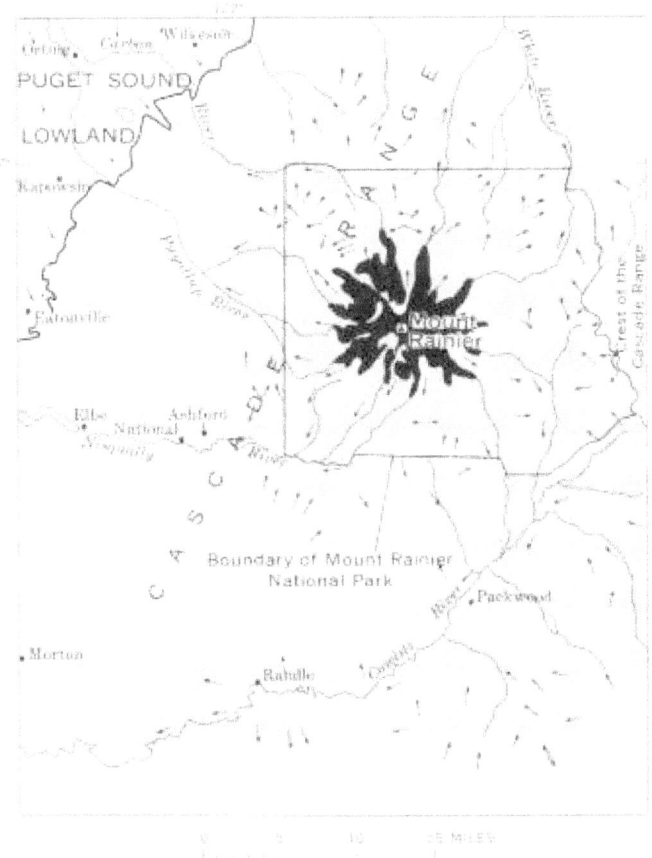

Extent of glaciers in the Cascade Range near Mount Rainier between about 15,000 and 25,000 years ago. Arrows show the direction of ice movement; solid black represents modern glaciers on Mount Rainier. (Fig. 16)

During the most recent major glaciation of the park, which lasted from roughly 25,000 to 10,000 years ago, ice again sheathed the slopes of the volcano, but glaciers in the nearby mountains were smaller than before. Most of the glaciers originated at the valley heads, where they gouged out countless bowl-shaped bedrock basins called **cirques**. Many of the basins held lakes after the glaciers disappeared. (See frontispiece.) Hikers on the trail to the Paradise ice caves cross the floor of a typical cirque at the head of Paradise Valley. From the Sunrise Visitor Center at Yakima Park you can walk a short distance to a point along the crest of the Sourdough Mountains and stand at the rim of a deep north-facing cirque. Ice originating in this cirque and in the cirques adjacent to it moved northward down the valley of Huckleberry Creek at least as far as the park's north boundary (fig. 16).

These glaciers left most valley walls in the park covered with rock debris. Lateral moraines can be seen along the highway at and just east of Ricksecker Point (fig. 17). Other glacial deposits are especially well displayed in roadcuts along the north wall of the White River valley.

Lateral moraine of rock debris at Ricksecker Point. It was formed by Nisqually Glacier when the glacier was at least 1,000 feet thick and about 15 miles longer than it is today. (Fig. 17)

A little more than 15,000 years ago the long glaciers began to shrink and recede. By 11,000 years ago there was only about as much ice on Mount Rainier as there has been within the last century. Then, during a short period of renewed glacier growth, most glaciers expanded short distances and new ones appeared in cirques from which ice had disappeared only a short time before. In some of these cirques so much rock debris was being dislodged from surrounding cliffs by repeated freeze and thaw that a **rock glacier**, consisting mostly of rock fragments bound together by ice, was formed. A trail to the Huckleberry Creek valley crosses hummocky rock debris left by such a rock glacier in a cirque on the southeast side of Mount Fremont. A larger rock-glacier deposit lies about 2 miles north of Sunrise Point in an east-facing cirque between The Palisades and Hidden Lake (fig. 18).

In other cirques, where the proportion of ice to rock debris was greater, the glacier transported the debris a short distance forward and built a terminal moraine. You can see particularly good examples of moraines formed about 11,000 years ago near Tipsoo Lake, where the pond southeast of the lake is dammed by a moraine, and at Mystic Lake. The ice that formed the terminal moraine at Mystic Lake was a tongue of Carbon Glacier.

In some places the orientation or altitude of the cirque did not permit enough snow to accumulate to form a glacier but just enough to create a permanent snowbank. Rock debris that fell from the surrounding cliffs rolled down these snowbanks and formed low ridges at their toes. Such a ridge is called a **protalus rampart** because it is found just in front of the apron of rock fragments, called **talus**, that lies beneath cliffs. A trail at Sunrise Point leads to protalus ramparts along the north side of Sunrise Ridge.

During the last 10,000 years, glaciers have been very small by comparison with the great ice mantles that overwhelmed the park earlier. However, glaciers have grown larger at least twice just within the last 3,000 years. During both of these periods most glaciers were slightly larger than they are today, and ice occupied most cirques at altitudes above 6,500 feet—even some that are now free of ice. The most recent time of extensive glacier growth began at least 800 years ago, and various glaciers in the park reached their maximum size between the mid-14th century and the mid-19th century. Oddly enough, even though all the glaciers headed on Mount Rainier, they did not all attain their maximum size simultaneously. The largest terminal moraine of this most recent glacial period was built by Emmons Glacier in the White River valley (fig. 19). It is now largely forested, and cores taken from the trees with a special boring tool that does not harm the tree show ages indicating that the moraine was stable enough to permit seedlings to survive on it by the mid-17th century. A similar but smaller terminal moraine built by Cowlitz Glacier has trees on it that started to grow in the mid-14th century.

Rock-glacier deposit (light-gray rubble beyond the brown slopes in the foreground) at The Palisades, which was formed about 11,000 years ago when the climate was colder than it is today. Rocks fell from the cliffs in such great quantity that a small glacier in front of the cliffs consisted of more rock debris than ice. The melting of the ice left a mass of broken rock several hundred feet thick which covers about 80 acres. (Fig. 18)

The hummocky end moraine at the left still had blocks of ice buried in it when this picture was taken in 1954. The front of Emmons Glacier was near the left edge of the bare moraine in about 1900. Now the glacier ends 1 mile farther upvalley at the upper right. The valley floor and moraine were buried by an avalanche of rock debris from Little Tahoma Peak in 1963. (Fig. 19)

Nearly all the glaciers gradually decreased in size after the mid-18th century. Although the shrinkage was sometimes interrupted by short periods of renewed glacier growth, by 1950 the glaciers at Mount Rainier covered only about two-thirds of the area that had been buried by ice only a century before. The overall loss of volume by Rainier's glaciers, as well as those elsewhere in the Pacific Northwest, was slowed or halted by slightly cooler temperatures and higher precipitation starting in the mid-1940's. Volume increases in their upper reaches caused the larger glaciers to grow from year to year, and since the early 1950's the terminuses of many glaciers have been advancing. This renewed growth of glaciers is not unique at Mount Rainier—similar changes have been observed at other glaciers in the Cascade Range and elsewhere.

Landslides and Mudflows—
Past, Present, and Future

Some of the most effective means of erosion at Mount Rainier are landslides and mudflows. Erosion of this kind is sometimes spectacular. Within an interval of only minutes or a few hours huge masses of rock may fall, slide, or flow off the volcano and move far downvalley.

Large landslides have occurred at many other places in the park—one in the area northeast of Mount Rainier is so conspicuous that its source has been named Slide Mountain. The ragged scar left by another slide near Grand Park is aptly called Scarface. You cross a slide on the Mather Memorial Parkway (U.S. Highway 410) just north of Cayuse Pass. Broken and jumbled rock debris of many sizes borders both sides of the highway there. This landslide broke loose in rocks of the Ohanapecosh Formation, slid downslope to the bottom of the valley, and dammed Klickitat Creek to form Ghost Lake. Rocks have also slid downslope on the west side of Backbone Ridge and on the east side of the Ohanapecosh River valley a short distance north of Ohanapecosh campground. The slide on Backbone Ridge is still slowly moving today. Another slide moves a few inches each year on the west side of the Nisqually River valley about 1 mile northwest of the visitor center at Paradise Park. You can recognize the slide by a jagged horizontal crack 1,000 feet long at its top.

A far more spectacular variety of landslide occurs when a mass of rock drops from a cliff to form a **rockfall**. The largest rockfalls on Mount Rainier in historic time occurred in December 1963 on the east flank. Masses of rock hundreds of feet across fell repeatedly from the steep north face of Little Tahoma Peak onto Emmons Glacier. The rock masses shattered into dust and countless fragments, fanned out across the glacier, then avalanched down the steep ice surface at tremendous speed. When the avalanches reached the end of the glacier they shot out into space as sheets of rock debris. As these hurtling sheets settled toward the valley floor, a cushion of compressed air formed beneath them, comparable to the air cushion that momentarily buoys up a sheet of plywood that is dropped onto a flat surface. Air that was trapped beneath these speeding avalanches reduced friction and permitted one of the avalanches to move almost 2 miles beyond the end of the glacier. This avalanche passed completely over a small wooden gage house about 5 feet high on the valley floor without damaging it, then ran headlong into the north base of Goat Island Mountain where it scraped away trees and bushes. A later avalanche stopped just short of the gage house, and wind that was expelled from beneath the rock debris blasted the still-undamaged house several hundred feet forward. It now rests in the scar left by the earlier avalanche on the side of Goat Island Mountain.

At least seven rockfalls and avalanches descended from Little Tahoma Peak, separated perhaps by only minutes or hours. The reddish-gray masses of broken and pulverized rock—some spread helter-skelter, some piled in long sharp-crested ridges—now lie on the valley floor between the White River campground and Emmons Glacier (fig. 20).

The rockfalls might have been caused by a steam explosion near the base of Little Tahoma Peak. Steam jets and small explosions are not unusual phenomena at Mount Rainier, although they never have had such dramatic effects in historic time.

Incredibly larger avalanches of rock fell repeatedly from the sides of Mount Rainier during prehistoric time. One such avalanche originated near the summit of the volcano and blanketed Paradise Park and Paradise Valley with a yellowish-orange mixture of clay and rocks sometime between 5,800 and 6,600 years ago. You can see this avalanche deposit in shallow cuts along trails and roads in the Paradise area. Huge blocks of rock that came down with the avalanche are scattered in the meadows of Paradise Park between the visitor center and Panorama Point. Although the deposit is now less than 15 feet thick in most places, the mass that flowed down Paradise Valley must have been 600 feet thick, because we can find remnants of it on top of Mazama Ridge. A tongue of the wet mass flowed through a low saddle near the south end of Mazama Ridge and extended into the basin now occupied by the Reflection Lakes. You can see the yellowish-orange deposit in the first roadcut west of the lakes, where it lies on top of gray glacial deposits.

Avalanche deposits in the White River valley. The rockfalls and avalanches from Little Tahoma Peak formed a mass of reddish-gray rock debris that contrasts with the darker gray glacial debris deposited

by Emmons Glacier within the last century. The avalanche deposits are about 1,500 feet across at their widest point. (Fig. 20)

The avalanche probably was wet when it crossed the Paradise area, and the moisture in it may have already been present in the rocks in which the avalanche originated. The mass was fluid enough to move down the Paradise and Nisqually River valleys as a mudflow hundreds of feet thick, and the resulting deposits extend at least 18 miles downstream from the volcano. The volume of rock that slid off to produce the mudflow may have been as much as 100 million cubic yards—or roughly enough to cover a 1-mile-square area to a depth of 100 feet.

At about the same time as the Paradise avalanche and mudflow occurred, a tremendous rock mass also slid off the east side of the volcano in the area between Steamboat Prow and Little Tahoma Peak. This slide formed a mudflow on the floor of the White River valley that was several hundred feet deep at the north boundary of the park and that extended at least 30 miles beyond the base of the volcano. The most remarkable feature of the deposit left by this mudflow is its surface, which is dotted with scores of mounds 5-35 feet high and as much as several hundred feet in diameter. These mounds have cores of huge rocks which are similar in size to those scattered on the surface of the avalanche deposits from Little Tahoma Peak. You can see the mounds best in an area which is a few miles north of the park boundary, west of the White River, and which can be reached by the Huckleberry Creek Forest Road. The total volume of this mudflow deposit may be as much as one-fifth of a cubic mile.

These great landslides and mudflows were followed shortly by another whose size surpassed that of anything before or since. This was the remarkable Osceola Mudflow, which streamed down the valleys of the White River and West Fork about 5,800 years ago. When these great rivers of mud joined in the White River valley, they formed an even larger mudflow which swiftly flowed downvalley for a distance of 15 miles and then spread beyond the Cascade mountain front into the Puget Sound lowland. There the mudflow submerged a total area of more than 100 square miles to depths as great as 70 feet and buried the sites of the present towns of Enumclaw and Buckley. One tongue of it even flowed into an arm of Puget Sound, south of Seattle, that has since been filled with river deposits to form the fertile valley occupied by the towns of Kent, Auburn, Sumner, and Puyallup.

The Osceola Mudflow is remarkable in that it affected areas so far from its place of origin. This long distance of travel was due to its great volume, which we estimate to have been more than half a cubic mile, and to the abundance of slippery clay in it. The clay had been formed by the alteration of rocks in the volcano by hot gases and solutions over many centuries.

The northeast flank of Mount Rainier. A remnant of the Osceola Mudflow lies at the summit of Steamboat Prow in the center. Two and one-half miles to the left is Little Tahoma Peak, from whose steep north face at least seven large masses of rock fell in 1963. Mount Adams volcano can be seen at the left, and Mount Hood, Oregon, in the far distance. (Fig. 21)

Where did the Osceola Mudflow originate on the volcano? This we must deduce from several lines of evidence. The mudflow occurred so long ago that there is no historical record, and volcanic events since that time have covered up part of the scar it left on the volcano. Remnants of the Osceola Mudflow veneer the sides and ridges of Glacier Basin, and a small amount of it is even preserved at the top of Steamboat Prow, at an altitude of 9,700 feet (fig. 21). This distribution tells us that the slides responsible for the mudflow originated somewhere on the volcano above Steamboat Prow. But now there is no great chasm in the side of the volcano large enough to have provided a source of the mudflow; so we must consider a former summit of the volcano itself as a possible source.

I. C. Russell, one of the first geologists to study Mount Rainier, wrote in 1896 that the present summit of the volcano consists of a small lava cone.

Enclosing this cone is a broad depression whose rim is partly preserved at Gibraltar Rock, Point Success, and Liberty Cap (fig. 11). High points on the rim indicate that the former summit of the volcano above an altitude of about 14,000 feet was removed in some way. The destruction of the old summit, which may have reached a height of 16,000 feet, left a broad east-facing depression in the top of the volcano between Gibraltar Rock and Russell Cliff. The depression has since been mostly filled by the recent lava cone. You can see these features best from high points east of the mountain.

Our best explanation of how the former top of the volcano was removed also solves the problem of finding an adequate source of material for the Osceola Mudflow. Before 5,800 years ago, the topmost part of Mount Rainier probably consisted of rock that had been weakened by hot volcanic fumes and solutions and partly converted to clay. Then, this mass of weak rock was jostled off or pushed off by a volcanic explosion and slid down the northeast side of the volcano. One or more of these mighty avalanches of moist clay and rock resulted in the Osceola Mudflow.

Large avalanches have also occurred many times during the last 3,000 years on the west side of the volcano. Sunset Amphitheater (fig. 11) is part of the large scar left by them. About 2,800 years ago one of these avalanches created a mudflow in the valleys of the South Puyallup River and Tahoma Creek that was temporarily deep enough to submerge Round Pass (on the West Side Road) to a depth of nearly 400 feet. This is especially remarkable when we see that Round Pass itself is 600-700 feet above the nearby valley floors. Another deep mudflow, started by an avalanche at Sunset Amphitheater, moved down the Puyallup River valley about 600 years ago and buried the site of the present town of Orting in the Puget Sound lowland under 15 feet of mud and rock.

TABLE 2.—*Summary of important geologic events in the history of Mount Rainier National Park*

Geologic time scale	Years ago	Geologic events in the area of the park
"Postglacial"		Present summit cone of Mount Rainier probably was built about 2,000 years ago. The last known pumice eruption occurred between 1820 and 1854.
		Glaciers started to grow and advance about 3,000 years ago. Maximum extents were reached about 1850 A.D. From then until about 1955, glaciers were receding; now they are in balance or advancing.

Huge masses of rock have slid from the volcano repeatedly during the last 10,000 years. One of these destroyed the summit of Mount Rainier and formed the Osceola Mudflow about 5,800 years ago.

	10,000	
Pleistocene (Ice Age)		Last major glaciation.
	25,000	
		Birth and growth of Mount Rainier volcano, and repeated glaciation.
	2-3 million	
Pliocene		Uplift and erosion of the Cascade Range.
	12 million	
Miocene		Intrusion of granodiorite.
		Folding of older rocks.
		Deposition of Fifes Peak and Stevens Ridge Formations.
	26 million	
Oligocene		Deposition of Ohanapecosh Formation.
	37-38 million	
Eocene		Deposition of Puget Group.
	53-54 million	

Avalanches and mudflows like those described are normal events at Mount Rainier and are expected to happen again in the future. Almost any cliff on the volcano can produce a large rockfall, but which cliff will collapse next, or when, cannot be predicted. Should the volcano again become active, earthquakes and volcanic explosions would trigger avalanches and mudflows that would rush down the mountain. Molten rock would melt snow and ice at the volcano's summit and send floods of water down the volcano's flanks. These indirect effects of an eruption would be much more hazardous than lava flows and pumice, if eruptions are on a scale similar to that of the past 10,000 years.

The Volcano's Future?

An active volcano changes continually. Repeated eruptions build the cone by piling one lava flow on top of others, or on top of other volcanic formations. Simultaneously, the combined processes of erosion wear the volcano down. The relative importance of the two processes—one building, the other destroying—is reflected in the volcano's shape. The scarred and deeply gouged sides of Rainier's cone show that erosion has been dominant here for a long time. Is Mount Rainier now doomed to continued piecemeal destruction until the lofty cone is reduced to a featureless mound? Will future eruptions of lava restore some of the volcano's bulk? Or will the volcano erupt violently some day, and then collapse as did Mount Mazama to form the deep basin of Crater Lake? The answers may not be known for centuries—or they may appear tomorrow.

Further Reading in Geology

Crandell, D. R., 1969, Surficial geology of Mount Rainier National Park, Washington: U.S. Geological Survey Bulletin 1288. A geologic map that shows where glacial deposits, landslides, and mudflows are located in the park is accompanied by an illustrated nontechnical description of these and other surficial deposits.

Crandell, D. R., and Fahnestock, R. K., 1965, Rockfalls and avalanches from Little Tahoma Peak on Mount Rainier, Washington: U.S. Geological Survey Bulletin 1221-A, 30 pages. A description of the seven successive landslides of December 1963 that buried the upper White River valley under thick deposits of rock debris.

Crandell, D. R., and Mullineaux, D. R., 1967, Volcanic hazards at Mount Rainier, Washington: U.S. Geological Survey Bulletin 1238, 26 pages. A discussion of Mount Rainier's eruptions during the last 10,000 years and the anticipated effects of similar future eruptions.

Fiske, R. S., Hopson, C. A., and Waters, A. C., 1964, Geologic map and section of Mount Rainier National Park, Washington: U.S. Geological Survey Miscellaneous Geologic Investigations Map I-432, with text. A geological map of the park's bedrock is accompanied by a brief nontechnical discussion of the geological evolution of the park as recorded by the rock formations.

Sigafoos, R. S., and Hendricks, E. L., 1961, Botanical evidence of the modern history of Nisqually Glacier, Washington: U.S. Geological Survey Professional Paper 387-A, 20 pages. A description of the recent moraines of several glaciers and an explanation of how they are dated by counting the growth rings of trees growing on them.

U.S. GOVERNMENT PRINTING OFFICE: 1968 O—353-560

Footnotes

[1] The X pumice occurs as scattered fragments and does not form a continuous layer.

[2] Ages of more than 150 and less than 6,000 years cited in this report are based on radiocarbon determinations which have been corrected by the use of a C_{14} half life of 5,730 years and for variations in atmospheric C_{14} (H. E. Suess, written communication to Meyer Rubin, 1968).

[3] For more information about glaciers read "Glaciers" by Robert P. Sharp, published in 1960 by the University of Oregon at Eugene.

Milton Keynes UK
Ingram Content Group UK Ltd.
UKHW040039180324
439604UK00006B/858